POINT OF ENTRY

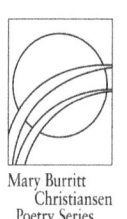

Mary Burritt
Christiansen
Poetry Series

Mary Burritt Christiansen Poetry Series
Hilda Raz, Series Editor

The Mary Burritt Christiansen Poetry Series publishes two to four books a year that engage and give voice to the realities of living, working, and experiencing the West and the Border as places and as metaphors. The purpose of the series is to expand access to, and the audience for, quality poetry, both single volumes and anthologies, that can be used for general reading as well as in classrooms.

Also available in the Mary Burritt Christiansen Poetry Series:

For additional titles in the Mary Burritt Christiansen Poetry Series, please visit unmpress.com.

POINT OF ENTRY

POEMS

KATHERINE DIBELLA SELUJA

UNIVERSITY OF NEW MEXICO PRESS | ALBUQUERQUE

ISBN 978-0-8263-6530-9 (paper)
ISBN 978-0-8263-6531-6 (electronic)

Library of Congress Cataloging-in-Publication data is
    on file with the Library of Congress

Founded in 1889, the University of New Mexico sits on the traditional
homelands of the Pueblo of Sandia. The original peoples of New Mexico—
Pueblo, Navajo, and Apache—since time immemorial have deep connections
to the land and have made significant contributions to the broader community
statewide. We honor the land itself and those who remain stewards of this land
throughout the generations and also acknowledge our committed relationship
to Indigenous peoples. We gratefully recognize our history.

Cover photograph by David Boca on Unsplash
Designed by Felicia Cedillos
Composed in Adobe Caslon Pro

The author wishes to recognize the poems that reference the border as poems
of witness. They are not intended to be claiming the voice of any specific
individual or group.

per la mia famiglia

To write about migration is, in a nutshell,
to write about humanity and the most ancient of customs.

—ADRIAN CASTRO

CONTENTS

POINT OF ENTRY

Desert Manifest

A doctor labors in Sonoran
heat, cataloguing bones.

The work is grueling.

Sometimes she whispers to the bones
rarely, they whisper back.

A group of bones occasionally found
together, but more often a femur

or an ulna, the long medial bone of the forearm
separated from the rest. Coyote, turkey vulture.

Its shaft is triangular.

And the desert is their ocean-faring ship
a list of names scribed across the sand

At the edge of sleep, some slim truth or partial answer
to her list of many questions.

So many without name or identification—

This isn't what she had trained for,
not what she had imagined.

Her classmates envied her dissections.
The secret: never ask the body to give up its truths alone.

Each bone is indexed and sent
to the state lab for genetic confirmation.

Let each one place an X upon the line beside their name

Not what she had imagined.
Coyote. Turkey vulture.

She thought her own practice, somewhere
her name would be known for midnight
house calls, kitchen-table consultations.

And the desert exhales its sail-wings
Moves its passengers forward

The doctor brushes dried blood
from a scapula that serves as origin
of the muscles that move the arm.

Let an accounting be done. An accounting done.

Border Patrol: Truth Be Told

Truth be told, entire days went by
without seeing anyone. Those were his favorites. Driving
la frontera. Sometimes he looked the other way. Truth be told,
his grandfather crossed in the '50s. Back when things were more relaxed,
no one thought twice about a few men running through the yard at night.
Trucks idling near the border. This was a good opportunity. Steady pay, benefits,
and he didn't mind the swing shift. Truth be told, he didn't speak English when he started school.
His parents steeped in the old ways. For weeks he walked the landscape of his classroom in a
haze. The smell of warm tortillas. Back when things were more relaxed between him and the
missus and the kids were still home, they came to the desert for picnics. Smell of warm creosote,
he didn't mind the swing shift. The entire night went by. He taught the kids to respect the rattler.
This was a good opportunity. Predators and how to track them.
Those were his favorites. His grandfather didn't speak English. *Cállate*, he called
from the bedroom window. Summer days running through the yard. Often, he looked
the other way. Trucks idling near the border. Steady pay, benefits. His grandfather worked
at the hospital, mopping the night-filled halls. Later it would be renamed environmental services.
No one thought twice.

All the Heroes Are Silent

after Anna Akhmatova

Pine needles, cholla branches, and water bottles.

The repeating blackwhite blackwhite
light through louvered walls, wire cages.

Don't dictate to me: I will transpose

    I will trespass

        I will seek asylum

The one people call spring, I call loneliness
The place you call dream, I call hopeful brutality.

Someone small has decided to live

Someone has decided to leave, to crawl
the drainpipe, scramble the trestle, crouch low
beneath mesquite.

Don't breathe: a shiver runs through the desert, a coyote whistles
in the dark.

One holds your life in his pocket. Nod of the head,
wink of his eye: you're part of the desert abandon.

    gravestones fragile
    granite softer than wax

See yourself searching a water station.
See yourself on your knees, hands clasped behind your back.

This is the kind of night where one must pay one's debts

I see dancing skeletons, I mark the desert with crosses.

Won't you say to me the word that conquers death?
Silence: speak.

Report from the Undertaker

To my shovel I am called with regularity.
So expert am I at the unearthing.

Ground soft or frozen, no matter.
Mothers cry at the openings
I have made:

*Demasiada, demasiada
la nena está cansada.*

In the family trade I followed
sleeves punched up with sweat and mud
my grandfather
passed me the shovel too large
for a boy of nine to grapple.

En sigues firme la vía.

What seems a muffling blanket
spreads to a kind of wail:

*El cielo se abrió,
la nena se cayó.*

I have learned the ways
of dirt and stone

how best to backfill
the hole

how gently
to settle the box.

Because Our Lives Are Small Fires
Buried under Dry Fields

after Tina Carlson

We run the length of furrows, dig deep
into mud and straw, peel
the casing from the seeds stored in the ground.
We soak
seed in our spit and shoot them
arrow-like against our bodies.

What does it mean to stand ground?
The tentative lawyer takes her place at the bar:

Yes, your Honor, my client is aware of her right to stand trial,
stand mute.
She has been informed of her civic duty.
She will not be painting the courthouse, gathering
trash, talking to children in the street.

The wind is a thin child's call and we wander farther afield.
Skies darken with bird wing, and harsh
from the tree
the raven is hidden but croaking.
The fox, his mouth filled with feathers.
The hawk circles the open again and again.

Here now, I'll take a stand, like the lawyer pleading her case:

What will it take to stop the humming,
the swirling. Hold steady.
Set the clock back three hours or a millennium.

Each small heaven so full of risk.

Each child wandering a field.
Each star bursting its case.

We Never Admit the Burden of
a Star Living in Our Chest

A glance, a gesture, and a door flies open.
A seven-layer dessert dripping with ganache appears on the
plate.

Oooo's and ahhhh's, I'm invited to all the parties.
I wear the same blue gown.

Rumor has it Houdini's wife wore the very one to all his
openings.
I leave that whispering to the others.

The wind tonight is a freight train.
Cat tails grow out of the desert, and my grandmother
erupts from the earth.

My shadow is a cat arching and whining.
And I am gagging and choking as if

on a hair ball, as if a celestial body.

Humanitarian Release

for Jakelin Caal Maquin

Or so it was called when they let her father
out of the holding center after she died.

A girl traveled hundreds of miles at her father's side
from their village home in Guatemala.

Soy un hogar para ti, her grandmother told her
as she filled the Dora the Explorer backpack:
hooded sweatshirt, water bottle, pink nightgown.

Humanitarian they call it when volunteers refill
the water stations scattered across the desert.

Her father carried her some part of the way.
He tossed her small body into the arms
of another traveler running alongside La Bestia.

We have no idea how to care for our own.

Did she believe her father when he said, *Tenemos que aprender
más constelaciónes?*
Nights walking the desert, her father telling stories about the
stars.

Somos estrellas muertes también,
a man in the cell next to her father said.

Dead stars still emit light over the desert.
Isn't that the definition of star?

To Be Carried This Way

The mother fox takes the kit
in its mouth

carries it to the bank of the river
moist tongue, teeth gentle
rough brush smoothing my fur-hair

    to be carried this way

dry patch my life, no blackberries along the shore
and the constant chore: silencing of the dead

    the mother fox carries its

so sure I would be a competent mother
I swore I would

    open, keep your mouth open, only a few more

worn path around a frozen pond, rusted spokes
wires curl at my feet

paddle boats placed upside down for the winter
certain I could skate without blades

    folds of moist

I live curled in the mouth of the fox
to you I'll say it again: the place

formed in the shape of a fox
ants crawl the pelt, ice-stare of its eye

and my brother hissing: *touch it, touch it, I dare you*

I Am Told Their Marriage Was Arranged

Her father agreed to the voyage
to appease the daughter whose future was settled.

The seas rough that spring,
she spent most of her time below deck.

A clear broth and the finest
hand-rolled orbs of meat.

Pasquale delivered the eggs every morning. She had moved
onto pastry by then.

Relaxed fingers and loose wrist
make an excellent whisk.

Her chafed hands difficult to hide at dinner.

Kidney beans soaked in caldo: *secret*
of her grandmother's soup.

The maître d' placed a placard in the window.

She never dreamed a woman
would be considered.

Her ossobuco caught the chef's attention.

Her aunt noticed the raw hands
but kept her questions to herself.

Late summer letters arrived: figlia quando torni.

Enriquetta inquired discreetly
about the young man who delivered the eggs.

Mi amorcito: Hoy vi algo en el desierto. No había nadie.
Yo caminaba paso a paso, mil pasos sin ti. Arena en mis ojos,
mis orejas, mi boca. Y allá en el medio del gran calor, un saguaro
enorme cubierto en cruces. Sobre las cruces, nombres tallados a mano.
Cada letra, roja, sagrada, sangrienta.

Carciofo

As the Dutch had carried it to King Henry's Court
and the French to Louisiana much later,
he carried it, a most precious thing,
in the aluminum Dutch oven before him.
His hands protected by insulated mitts,
he carried it like the gift it was.
This spiky unreachable.
This inflorescent cousin of thistle,
the plant that grew wild in the fields and sandy soil
in the Sicilian hill town where he was born.
He was fourteen when his father sent him west
across the Atlantic
into the hands of friends of friends.
Stranni, his mother complained as she wrapped
a small loaf of bread and a rind of cheese into a linen cloth.
His father sent him
in search of something more
to this place across the sea.
He would find that more and make it better still.
With a handshake and a paper bag
of paper money
he would buy land and profit.
Build a few shops.
Grow the new world, a wife and a son,
and his son would too.
Until this night
when my grandfather walks the few suburban steps to our house,
past the leaning willow Mr. Hickey refuses to cut down,
past Mrs. Schera's yard filled with English roses.
He steps carefully over the uneven square of cement
pushed forth by the unruly

roots of sycamore. The glowing silver pot
filled with the manna of his childhood.
Hand stuffed for his son's family.
A precious thing made more so by its inner secret.
Its soft and delicate heart protected by a wreath of spiny thorns
sharp enough to draw blood from the thumb of a careless cook.
The layered green leaves
filled with garlic and breadcrumbs
just as his mother had shown him
despite his father yelling from the garden,
Ho bisogno di quel ragazzo qui,
demanding the boy come now.
Green with parsley and overflowing with grated Romano.
Roman steps, his steps.
Along this New Jersey street, carrying the steaming pot
to our front door.

In Your Letter
You Asked about Ceremony

I can tell you I carried water to nurses on a picket line
one translucent bottle placed in every palm.

I can tell you believers burn the palms
of Easter and store them for another year.

I can tell you I stood at my brother's grave that year
and watched as his ashes were interred.

I have crossed sterile water on a newborn's head.
I have crossed old names from mailboxes.

I can tell you my family lived with silt-soaked mailboxes
frayed altar cloths and soggy cardboard

gifts of the hurricane
Gloria, I believe.

I have read that ceremony requires an oath or declaration.
Ritual has no such matter.

Monastery in the Desert, Abiquiu, New Mexico

A man carries a cross
tipped sideways
as if about to fall
from his shoulder his back
from the chapel wall where blood drips irregularly
but it's blood just the same.

On the day we finally came to the monastery
hidden deep in the tertiary age.
Layers of colored ribbons of rock
yellow mustard terracotta cream.

Taking the curves slowly or a little fast
until the high-sloped curve that tipped a bit too much over the
green Chama water
and we both said at the same moment, *What if someone . . . ?*

So we slowed down
because what else is there really to do
when the ruts cut deeper and the quiet more intense.

By the river, a sandy beach looking something like Coney Island
but I'm talking long ago.

We moved along the thirteen miles of twist and dirt and rut
and entered a small parking area and the deepest quiet yet.
Geese lifting off the river, the wind blowing cold and blue.

In the chapel, a monk praying.
Light falling in squares across the stone altar
the white altar cloth moving gently in a waft of radiant heat.

And way up there, at the top of the cliff
two crosses and five crows.

Such Is the Story of Leaving

for Gustavo

If the invasive eucalyptus were in season.
If the radio were playing the Stones instead of Gardel.

How would he have known there'd be no *tormenta*.
If he packed the wrong clothes for the season.

July and the eve of his birthday.
Andá al norte, circling his head.

If it was humid would he have noticed.
His friends had promised to come.

Drop in his stomach as the jet lifted, day his third niece was born.
Such is the story of leaving.

Brash smell of hot dogs and weak coffee.
A basket lined in canvas or coiled to look like a hive.

The list he kept in his pocket: cassette tapes, shoelaces, *panadería*.

To watch movies in your adopted language is to lull yourself from
the truth.
Such is the story of survival. An army blanket, a spare room for
rent.

If someone said, *clambake* or *mini-mart*.
If someone said, *I'll bring a six*.

How little of the language he commanded.
Someone said, *I'll make the nachos.*

Como si esa cadencia nunca antes la hubiera escuchado.
If the cadence was like nothing he'd heard.

My Grandfather Teaches Me
How to Flay the Heart

It was considered ritual in our family.
The cleaning of the spiny thistle.

A passing
of tradition and knowledge.

The confidence
that one could handle the blade, as well as the spine.

Catarina, my grandfather calls, *questo è come è fatto.*
This is how it's done.

And with thorny heart in one hand
and blade in the other

he teases apart
the layers, each leaf nested tight within the next.

The spiny thorns grow sharper with progression toward the heart.

He left his heart in the sandy soil of his Sicilian hill-town home
the day he boarded the ship that would take him west across the sea.

Sitting at his kitchen table, he passes me the layered heart
with strong warning: never leave a single thorn in place.

A teasing out, a gentle splay.

My grandfather's hand on mine.
His shoulder solid for me to lean on.

A stone wall built around a small village.

Caceroleada

Sin luz

The strike was an idea spread by no one. The strike caught on in a flash. One night a few sailors bragging over beer and the next thing you know. The city had been losing power for an awfully long time. The residents tired of darkness. What use a lightbulb without juice? How to keep the humidifier running when the children had croup? How could they count all the chickens?

Con fuerza

The man in the chef's hat was tired of striking. He'd been striking for an awfully long time. When the order came to strike, the chef took the order quite seriously. He struck it at noon, he struck it at dinner, he occasionally struck after midnight. In the morning, others came out to strike. Some holding soup pots, some holding colanders, some holding their heads.

Caldo

The pot was tired of being struck. It wanted simply to fall apart. But the pot was made of cast iron. And we know what they say about iron. A worn spot was the recipient of all the striker's attention. Wooden spoon, spatula, miniature hockey stick. A weariness filled the pot and spoiled the kidney-bean soup. What soup can resist the flavor of weary?

Letter to My Suegra from Artesia, New Mexico

It's easier to cross the babies one at a time
on inner tubes or rafts,
that way, I notice if one goes under.

—*Anonymous coyote*

Querida suegra, They're holding Dora and the children in jail, Dora and so many children. Children who've traveled north in the shadows and trusted coyotes to be their guides.

You remember Dora, don't you, *suegra*? The little brown girl with the pet monkey named Boots. The girl who says *lo hicimos* and *unodostres*. Her face everywhere here, on sneakers, on Band-Aids, on bathing suits and water bottles. And now behind barbed-wire fences, nine feet high.

Nothing like *el muro* on Tiburcio Gómez all the *sobrinos* loved so much. Remember them leaning on the wall in the evening, waiting for Don Lorenzo to turn out the light? Gustavo and Alvaro would climb *la parra*, reaching for the sweetest, darkest grapes. Stretching out so far they almost brought the whole *viña* down. Rinsing fruit for days was their penance, while Don Lorenzo's sons crushed *las uvas* beneath their feet.

No grapes here for the children to cram their mouths full. No sneakers or water bottles for these children brought to the banks of the Rio Grande and told to swim right to the uniformed men. Thrashing their arms, flapping their mud-stained feet.

The Function of Walls

In some ceremonies the medicine man will use a badger's claw or paw

*Fatigue, pathologic, longitudinal, spiral, compression, oblique,
greenstick, comminuted, transverse, simple, compound*

A gate, more of an arbor with a door

Technique is all

An additional tablespoon or two to reach the desired consistency

*For the present, all that needs to be said: DNA resembles a tape
subdivided into units*

*It is elastic, rugged, and under ordinary circumstances self-generating,
more common than its cousin the raven*

Those who are gone, those who remain, migrate at night in flocks

*Raven is much more shy
requires a cavity for nesting*

*The clouds hang low, and I can only think of the border
call upon coyote and the function of walls*

De la tormenta: Desert Survival

I choose who will kowtow
at water barrel or cool mouth
of mountain lion.

I decide who will huddle
beneath mesquite

lungs haunted by river water
sandmites bursting the skin.

No handpicked cosmic joke
slicked down from desert sky.
This took centuries to negotiate.

Kestrels like chocolate on my tongue.
Who do you think was speaking
when you heard, *Beware the ditch?*

No promises, no portents
nothing savory or sweet.
This is no gift wrapped in sage.

A man floats in the river
a child arrives at the border.

One must manage what one has created.

Come, sit beside me on this leather console seat
the carriage that honors so many will carry you across.

That figure in cloak and biretta cap
he will manage the horses.

Border Patrol: Por supuesto

Por supuesto, it was the day of his supervisor ride along. A mother, a father. Three children. He turned his truck the other way. *Por supuesto*, they headed for the water station. Maybe he grabbed her too hard. The baby wouldn't stop screaming. Day of his supervisor ride along. It's not that his work was in question; sometimes these things had to happen. Sand in the cracks of the truck bed. No diapers, no milk. The baby screaming. *Por supuesto*, he could translate, he grew up speaking the language. Some heard screaming, some only wanted a drink. *Por supuesto*, they notified the authorities, an agent read them their rights. Someone pulled out a cell phone. Did he grab her a little too hard? It's not that his work was in question. He'd just returned from vacation. Took the wife down to South Padre. The ocean waved at his feet. Sand in the cracks of the truck bed. Some only wanted a drink. One agent was talking to the children, one grabbed for the baby's feet. The mother wouldn't stop crying. *Por supuesto*, the vans went in opposite directions. He circled back to the station. It's not that his work was in question. The ocean still waved at his feet. Sometimes these things had to happen.

How to Lose One Thousand Four Hundred
Seventy-Five Children

First, let there be children.
A mountain of children.

Elena. Maria Teresa. Tomás.

And because every story starts somewhere,
let's say these children begin in Tegucigalpa, San Salvador, Chiapas.

Let's say they travel through jungles, across borders, ride an iron
dragon.
Say there are coyotes, a river, and uniformed men.

Let the men gather the children.
The children cry and cough, the men sweat and wheeze.

Let the men be overwhelmed by children.
Enrique. Alejandro. Estrella.

Next, come those who work for the state.

Some carry clipboards and cell phones.
Some, orange juice and diapers.

Let them collect the children into vans.
Let the vans jump and twist across the sand.

Little ones lulled to sleep in the front,
the bigger ones sick in the back.

Let them arrive at the prison that once was a barracks.
Let it be midnight and windswept, let floodlights scurry the sand.

Let the night shift.

Never mind paper.
Forget about pens.
Forget to wake up
the translator.

So if it happens that no one
is paying attention, if it happens that no one writes down the name
of sponsor, of guardian, next of kin.

Javier. Claudia. Jorge.

Or if it is written on the back of an envelope,
a manilla folder, a brown paper bag
that later ends up in the trash.

If the only name they are given is *unaccompanied alien child*.

Then what of Nalleli. Esteban. Marisol.
Luisa. Osvaldo. Jesus.

¿Qué le pasó a Patricia. Fernando. Juan Andres?

Unsigned Affidavit

Not the phone number sewn inside the dress.
Not the thunderhead of smoke, orange tinged.
Not the child's pink flip-fops abandoned.

Torn t-shirt draped on a cholla.
Baby doll missing its arms.
Bloody socks. Bloody sneaker.
Two dirty diapers rolled in a ball.

Empty water bottle

empty water bottle

empty water

Point of Entry

I can be anywhere when it happens.
Sliding from the roof, just returning from flight.

The pressure
as if from the palm of a hand.
It can be anytime.

As dusk is descending, in between sleeps.
A firm but steady push, propulsion through the wrist.
Behind my right shoulder, at the base of the bony plate.

There, a wing emerging.

My Grandmother Told the Story This Way

She was flying above the Palisades, watching the colors of sunset fall over the river. She could see the entire valley and the way the river sliced through the land. My grandmother jumped awake. All seemed quiet in the house. The clock my grandfather carried from Luino ticked softly above the stove. His sleep-breathing syncopated to the ticking. The lights of a passing car outside the window briefly lit up the wall of their room. And there, at the foot of their bed, a soft radiant figure. A woman wrapped in a translucent blue cloak.

The air around her seemed to glow. My grandmother was certain she smelled roses. The woman called softly, *Sara, Sara,* in a voice so familiar, a northern Italian lilt. She had never been so awake. She felt the air on her skin prickling. She remembers the heater cycling on, my grandfather shifting slightly in his sleep.

Your brother will be healed, he is safe, the glowing woman at the foot of the bed told her. And that was all. My grandmother blinked and rubbed her face and watched as the figure dissolved into the floral wallpaper and the sapphire light from the window.

In the morning, the telegram arrived.

Letter from the Sky: Dear Border

A line of buttons, a box of old coins
from here, you are nothing.
Paper money someone's grandmother
might have saved
after the market crashed.
From here I see you are delible.
What's all the fuss over landlines?
You are rows and rows of actuarial table.
A percentage calculated from a distance. You are frayed.
You come undone with the hint of a run on the market
or a stiff breeze. Why bother to invest at a time like this?
Why hurry to bolster your defenses?
There are miles enough for everyone, down to the smallest child
walking shoeless in the desert, trying so hard to avoid the thorns.

Postmortem Variations

when coyote appears quite often something unexpected and unwelcome will occur

To ask would have been rude,
details of how and when.
To discuss color and viscosity, the odor
and yet isn't that what we want?
Terror and fascination
draw us to the fire and the gorge.
We gorge on tidbits, ogres that we are.

> *bones in the desert*
> *story of refuse laid bare*
> *water station slashed open and empty*
> *the Sonora refuses nothing*

> *coyote is not a pack animal*

To splay the fascia requires patience,
no value in a hurried job.
Cut flap, pin edges, expose
entrail, sclera, and bone.
Come: feast.

Amor de mi vida: sigo caminando hacía al norte. Paso a paso, por esta tierra sin fin.
Busco la estrella que es mi guía como lo eres tú para mí. Los animales del desierto salen en la
noche. Hay otros durante el día: los hombres que llegan de uniforme. Ellos puedan hacerme mucho
más daño. Durante todas las noches tan oscuras, tu corazón es mi estrella.

It took weeks
to occupy the body
expanding into digits was a task
by the time winter had settled
it seemed I had a corporeal home

coyote is spoken of in some books and predictive systems as the bringer
of hard lessons

The thinnest vein can withstand the least pressure.
Threading a catheter into the vessel
one must wait for the sign of entry: the smallest, lightest pop.

coyote likes to sing, enjoying a night chorus as much as the wolf

O bones
They call and crumble in the heat. Sand
in the feet, ears thrumming. Desert wind.
They call. Sleep in the day. Move quickly at night.

Tortita, tortita,
tortita de manteca
para mamá que le da la teta.

Para papá que no le da nada.

In the Drawer of My Grandmother's
Writing Desk, the Dead Rest

They appear in the shape of a stack
of small cards, softened from age and handling.
Smelling faintly of lavender and garlic.
Cream colored with gray lettering and images
of aunts and uncles I never knew: Uno, Antonio, Regina Felice.
The slightest smile on their faces,
or no smile at all but a reflection
of light in their eyes.

In this way I came to know those who had come before.
I began to understand my place
in the line of the daughter of this daughter
of this daughter's son.
Some who had traveled across the sea,
others who had stayed behind.
Back when the onionskin envelope
with the red and blue edging seemed so exotic
and yet usually heralded sad news.

When the crackling voice of the overseas
operator meant only one thing: another loss.
Another cream-colored card to add to the pile.
Because wouldn't they want to be together?
Wouldn't the ancestors find comfort
together at that large oak table standing somewhere in a field?
Cavatetti and steaming bowls of marinara,
sliced tomatoes and mozzarella.
The uncles sharing a few cigars,
the aunts, morsels of gossip.

Don't they laugh, aren't they amused
as they watch us scurry to place
flowers at their graves, honor their saint days,
light candles, waiting for some small sign:
tap on the shoulder, knock at the door,
bowl of ziti knocked to the floor?
How they love to play us.

Consider the Night

Mussel shells ground with blackbird wings produce the hue of evening.
The underbelly of trumpet mushroom offers a shade of dusk.

> *Consider the craft.* Rows of hand-sewn pieces, threadbare days, fat quarter nights.

She would baste and turn, recall her grandmother's swollen ankles, years of pedal and pump.
A friend in Antonito saved the wool of every black lamb.

> *Consider the craft.* Pierce deep the midnight layer.
> *Consider the heartbeat,* slight shiver of the stitch, the pulse at her wrist.

Ink of the bobtail squid leaves her fingers stained for weeks, smudges on every glass in the house.

> *Consider the curve of snail shell,* the obsidian thread that runs.

To relieve the ache. Her grandmother asked for help.
She sat on the floor and pulsed the pedal with her hands.

> *Consider the heartbeat,* its constant soothing drum.

She spent hours in the quiet of table legs and chair. Charm squares of white bread, thimbles of water.

Her grandmother said the best work often goes unseen.

I Am Told Her Parents Knew Nothing of the Plan

They saved for months
ever since Cesare's letter announcing his springtime arrival.

The neighbor's curtains parted slightly in the evening
when Pasquale walked her to the door.

Her aunt's raised eyebrows.

By then she had relinquished her old life
the kitchen was her new one.

She developed a series of dipping sauces: parsley, garlic oil, poached
truffles
each named for a different family member.

Arriving early at the pier, they watched the ship's slow approach
the evening loaves waited by the oven.

How to explain to her betrothed, his wasted weeks at sea.
She had a plan, and the Old World had no part.

Cesare swayed down the ramp
spotted her waving, Pasquale's hand at her elbow.

His accent surprised her. Piccolina, he called.
His outdated Piedmonte clothes.

Enriquetta and Pasquale passed Cesare
an envelope
filled with their savings.

He looked down and spit at their feet.

Your Grandmother's Bolognese

Don't begin if you're angry.
A relaxed jaw is needed
to mince.
Ask for an ancestral blessing:
touch knife blade
to worn whetting stone.
Your tears will moisten the onions
add a little less
salt. Stir deep into the pot
or something will surely get singed.
Fold in tomatoes once.
Remember the sugar for St Gertrude.
If your grandfather appears, use oregano.
It will always taste better on Thursdays.
Add a T-bone if you wait until Sunday.
It should smell like the moment
you stepped into her house.
In her village, *sprutti* means
beginning to thicken.

On the Day I Order My Ancestry Kit,
I Also Order Scopa Cards

Or what sounded to me like *scuba*
or *scoopuh* when my grandparents said it.
Something Sicilian and covered in sesame seeds.

But no, it was the table that was covered in crumbs
because crackers were a part of our scoring system.

And although I know the names of the parents of my grandparents
and the names of their villages too—*Cerami, Piverone, Masenzana*—
I am searching for something more.

Did my ancestors sail from Tunisia or Greece or Spain?
Were they indentured or bartered, convicts runaways gadabouts?
Were they sailors willing or not, swaying on the deck playing scopa,
a game with small cards or dice or carved bone? Something to pass
the time,
to challenge to bet: *uno, due, tre.*

Did they throw away their earnings or throw someone
over, because what else is there to do when your watch is done?
You've choked down a crust of flat bread with a bit of salt fish and
stale water.

I take another sip of cool water and spit into a small plastic tube,
fill the tube to the blue wavy line, wait six weeks for answers.

In the bright-yellow breakfast nook
that was part of my grandfather's kitchen, I held those scopa cards
tight.
Scooping the deck, calling the points: *uno, due, tre.*

My grandmother would pause the game when the saltine
crumbs threatened
to take over the table, and then it would be time for a few
cookies,
maybe a glass of milk. A dark espresso for my grandfather.

He'd reach over and pinch my cheek,
thumb and finger, with an extra hard twist
and he'd say my name, *Catarina*, like no one else ever did.

We the Dead

the dead there did not dance, they had something better to do

—*H. C. Andersen*

Unsew the seam, unshoe the foot.
We are busy decomposing.
Uproot the tree that wraps
simple boxes swell and shift. Rattle
the bones boxofbones.
Night crawlers of story, trawlers
of mushroom, earthworm and mole.
We dead have so much more than worry.
In the churchyard
unclutter the tomb, unhum the tune,
unwind linen, unfracture bone.
Here in the ground never done.
Untalking, undancing, unstitching the story.
What is left will root or rot,
grow or not grow,
give harvest or decompose.

Open the seam. Tear the thread.

Querida: Agarré a la Bestia. Un monstruo. Había momentos que pensé que no iba ha sobrevivir. Así es. Un montón de gente corriendo al lado del dragón. Algunos se cayeron. Una chiquita no pudo agarrarse. Desapareció y no quiero saber que fue de ella. Esta noche estoy rezando por tí y por la chiquita también. Ojalá que ella siga viva. Ojalá que todavía tenga dos piernas, dos pies.

Freight Train

Freight trains run the night, through the center of our town. Township, part of its formal name, but I always found that a little standoffish. *Stand off the rails,* my brother yells as he balances copper pennies on the track. Tracks run clearly down the center of his arm, and I know it will be a long night. Night comes with the roar of crickets and the flash of fireflies. Fire flies from the rails as the speeding train crushes the coins flat. Flat on our backs, we stare up at the singing wires. Wires, soda cans, and old newspapers blow through the tunnel under the rails. Railing against the stink, we run hand in hand, jump the dank puddles. Puddles led to other dark places. One day my brother fell in. In my version of his life, he toured with Jimmie, played backup for Janis, his name written among the great ones. One by one I pull apart the tangles, stare myself down hard in the mirror. Mirror to him, I crack open another bottle. Bottle thrown at a brick wall, *This is the way to work rage*, he told me. He told me, *Take another hit*, right before everything blurred. Blurred like an Etch a Sketch drawing, shake it hard up and down, start again.

The Joy of the Moment Turns Suddenly into a Black Hood with Openings

after Adam Zagajewski

A tunnel opens beneath our lives
and like the little girl in the pinafore dress
we fall and fall.
We pass ourselves in the falling.
See our bodies reflected in mirrors and sinkholes
as we fall farther still.
All void, null and void.
We grow accustomed to the falling
and the pressure growing against tympanic membranes.
This tunnel steeped in darkness.
Once we found the entrance, there was no looking back.
And now we live as if we might never see light again.
We are parched for light, famished for light.
Cry out amid our falling.

For One Brief and Shining Moment
She Held the World in Her Body

The tiny zygote was everything. Every ancestor, doorknob, bowling alley, tight rope. Every grandmother, every hand-sewn shawl. She was strong and royal and glorious. She could take on any challenger of the universe and ride the Loch Ness monster home. The small collection of cells would grow in her, in her! How could it be that she would become a universe to this miniature magus-superhero growing deep inside, taking root within her hermitage, her sanctuary, her imperial city. The clump of rapidly dividing cells, dividing now, and now, now, now. At least eight times since she saw the blue plus on the urine-dipped wand. Each division growing the zygote recessed in her private garden into something more. Involution, differentiation. All this happening in her as she ate a bagel, opened an umbrella, stepped into a new pair of boots. She was Her Royal Highness Queen Majestic with direct lineage back to Eve, Lilith, Noah's wife. She was species manifestor. 3D printer of humanity. She held the copyright for every infant that would ever come forth again: and then the blood came.

Three Angel Studies

One

The angel coveted the roof of the house she was assigned to. Her chest pressed against the tarry surface, her arms wrapped protectively around the walls, hands resting gently on viga stubs. The humming sound of family life reverberated her ear. They were her own. She was smitten. At night, she relaxed her hold, a bit. At noon, she escalated the movement of her wings, sending a current of cooling air rolling over the home. Hers for thirty days, well, technically, twenty-eight. But she always hung around for an extra day or two to make sure the soul was firmly settled into the newborn body.

Two

The angel coveted the roof of the house. She had been doing flyovers for months, waiting. Now as she wrapped her arms around the walls, the fresh smell of amniotic fluid engulfed her. She sensed the mother's milk ducts expanding. Millennia of neonatal guarding had taught her the tenuous hold of the soul in a newborn body. If one slipped out before its time, she could usually track it to a loss of concentration. The slightest interruption in her focus, and that soul could squeeze right out of any available aperture. Early in her tenure, she hadn't known the free floaters could be so wily. Generally, the soul was accepting of its new position. But every so often, one came along that had no interest whatsoever in pulling on the robe of blood and bone again.

Three

The house sighed. Every few years a new child, another angel.

Generally, the house didn't mind, it did give her a bit of a break. Not easy to stand plumb and tall, year after year. Beams need to stretch sometimes. Occasionally roofs don't mind a day off. Whether it was the same angel each time or not, the house couldn't tell. A light so bright surrounding its face, it was difficult to make out any features at all. But she was good company. And vigilant. Once, a hailstorm came up so rapidly the house barely had time to square its walls. Yet the angel puffed her chest, billowed her gown into the largest tent the house had ever seen. Not a hail pock or scratch on the gutter after the storm had passed. The house had only respect for a being that solid and determined.

House Made of Fog and Goodwill

Dear Tina,
For a time, my grandfather built houses.
He had a partner who did the actual building,
but my grandpa bankrolled, supervised, gave opinion.
Ada and Natalie built a *small intricate house out of breath and distance.*
You and I know that house.
Those are the rooms in which we thrive.

Smell of wet plaster, I thrive on.
If I could, I'd build houses and move and move.
Rearrange the furniture, roll down the hill in the back.
But that was my grandpa's yard, with a small hill on the side, corner lot.
In summer, the neighborhood kids met there after dinner.
No parents in the way. In the thick summer of the east coast,
hours of light left. We sat on that little hill
and threw clots of dried dirt at tires of passing cars.
We sat as crickets awakened. Streetlights warmed.
Sycamores sighed our mothers' distant calls.

Lament for Joaquin Macias

It was 5:00 a.m. when the rumbling started.
Señora Alvarez carried her laundry to the yard.
Un camión broken down on the street.

7:00 a.m., the next tremor shook the tiles from the roof,
families on the upper floors scrambling.

8:00 p.m., Joaquin slammed the door after picking a fight with
his *mujer*.
Her red dress and the neighbor's stare.

She sent him to sleep with the dogs.
Afuera, afuera, anda afuera, residents on the higher floors
screaming.

It was 8:45 p.m. when Joaquin checked into the Motel 6 on West
15th,
thought nothing of showing the small, laminated square
when the front desk clerk asked for ID, his driver's license from
Mexico.

At midnight, the meteorologist called the presidential palace:
*Un temblor como nunca visto antes. Better move to the bunker, safer
there.*

1:00 a.m., the front desk clerk faxed the guest list to ICE.

At 2:30 a.m., agents jammed their feet in the door,
searched him and read him his rights.
Cuffed him and hustled him to the van.

And there was a temblor from deep inside
and the smell of his mother's corn masa:

His brothers stole her comal
from the kitchen, smuggled it out to the yard.
A paste made of ants, eggshell, and cricket,
daring their hermanito: go on, take a bite.

In the Pima County
Medical Examiner's Office

The dead do not rest.
They wait.

Border Response [Deconstructed]

These facilities [detention centers] do not automatically appear [liquidate another business]. When people [with brown skin] arrive [barely alive] at the border [artificial man-made delineation]. They [the prisons] are not permanent [not welcome] structures [no plumbing, no heat]. It takes time [money] to construct [prefabricate] facilities [prisons], hire people [mercenaries] and wait [watch FOX News] for Congress [the devil you know] to act [make a profitable deal]. Our laws [corporate incentive] entice them [brown people] to come [place their lives in the hands of a stranger] and then cause them [no other choice] to expect [plead for] certain kinds of care [blankets, water, bread].

Legend of the Compassionate Brigade

The squadron was legendary. Their skills impressive.
Intense concentration and intricate synchronization.
Their gift: the ability to stare into the eyes of their foes,
persuading them to lay down their arms.
Chest to chest. Slow the breath.
Weapons placed at their feet.

Many of the members reported childhood obsessions
with winged creatures, cell biology, and the mechanics of lifting
immense objects. Many spoke multiple languages,
their bodies fluent in martial arts.
They drilled constantly.

No active recruitment was needed.
Members were drawn to the squadron. An article,
a snippet of ballade or story, and they'd arrive.

The patch on their uniform: an open palm, lifeline sliced.
A dove breaching out of the wound.

Cesare's Gift

after Roethke

He was already back on board the ship when he realized he hadn't given her the gift. O Piccolina! He had carried the little bird all the way from Lago Maggiore. Guarding her carefully. Crumbling crusts of bread for her back in his berth. It was a ridiculous idea, but he had wanted to surprise Riquetta. A sparrow from home arriving here, in the New World, with him! The young men in his village smirked as they heard his plans: *Allora? Vai a riprenderti la tua donna scappata?* His arrival was like nothing he had imagined, *the spirit still wet from its bud sheaths.* Days on the open ocean, the achingly slow approach to shore, the gulls calling her name, *Rrriiiiii, Rrrriiiiii, Rrrrriiiii.* By the time he reached the gangplank, *his stomach was an old woman jumping in her shoes.* The Piemonte sparrow, *a sentry of seeds*, restless in his pocket. Aroma of unknown foods and names being called out in so many different languages. A white handkerchief waving to one side of his view. And she was there. Enriquetta, looking so much more mature and confident. So much like the New World, he'd realize later. Cesare's eyes moved slowly from his betrothed to the paisano, standing bold and tall at her side. *Disgraziato*, his hand on her elbow! He knew before he reached them on the dock. *Once I was sweet with the light of myself*, Cesare thought. Small waves knocking against the cement retaining wall, a few mumbled introductions, and then a fat envelope shoved into his hands. The only thing he could do was turn around and walk right back up the ramp. *His flesh was breathing slower than a wall* when he reached his berth, and of course the crew were already there cleaning. He asked vaguely how to purchase a ticket home and then realized he had enough for an entire stateroom if he wanted it. When they passed the green lady that stood guard over the harbor, he heard her say, *Hai sprecato la tua vita.* The shifting midnight air led him to the deck that night. *And dreams came closer*, he whispered to the sparrow as he pulled the sleeping bird from his jacket and opened his hand.

To Be Part of Something Complete and Great

for Camila

As that stunning release
when your newborn pushes headfirst into her life
yells at the sharp snap of lung sails unfurling.
The cord still pulses and she is unfolding
already too large to return to that cushioned grotto.
You are both covered in salt—
she the amniotic brine, you the tears of your labor.
She is offered to you a coffer of living myrrh
and as she mews and searches the truffle of your breast
you pull her close and whisper to this future you will suckle,
You are most welcome.

I Ask My Grandmother to Repeat the Story

She takes a small breath and begins again
to tell the story of my grandfather arriving in this country.
He was young and traveled alone and almost ended
up in Buenos Aires like his sister,
but that ship had left port the day before.

And though it is my grandmother's nap time
and her afternoon fatigue has set in,
the tremor of her left hand
rapping a rhythmic backdrop
on our wooden kitchen table,
still she doesn't say no.
Her pale-blue cardigan dances
with her northern Italian blue eyes.

My grandfather arrived in New York with no English
and no directions to his uncle's home.
Carrying only the words his father had given him.
He asked all who might understand, *Dieci mosci? Dieci mosci?*
Searching for his uncle and his future,
when finally a paisano made the connection: *Dieci mosci!* Ten flies!

Il paisan' directed my grandfather
to the ferry that took him across the Hudson River
and then a train on the Jersey side to his uncle's town: Tenafly.

I laughed every time, and now I know that was why

my grandmother never refused a retelling of the story.
A small flame lit up in her northern blue eyes,
and a soft chuckle rocked her shoulders and thin frame.
She'd take another sip of her tea, sigh,
and ask me to help her to bed.

Poem with a Writing Studio and
a Cherry Tree Growing from Within

We had moved in that dream way
where you can be in a brand-new place and still be right at home.
We were touring the house. Everything seemed new and sparkling
even though the house itself was old and still filled
with many items precious to and well used
by the elderly man who had lived there before us.
There was a mustard-yellow corded phone
hanging on the kitchen wall, notes left in his office,
and a screened-in front porch for warm summer nights.
And for Halloween, decorating that would scare
the neighborhood kids just enough to let them know
there was a new family in the old man's house.
I was asking our newer older neighbor,
Do you decorate for holidays here, and she nodded her head
in that wise-woman way as I passed a yellow bowl
to my daughter and asked her to pick cherries from the tree
that was growing right in the middle
of the house but also in the courtyard
out the kitchen window. The tree was filled
with cherry blossoms and fully ripe fruit.
I invited our neighbor to tour my writing studio.
A small casita in the deep-green yard. It had multicolored shutters
and stained-glass windows and seemed to me a treasure chest.
Its walls could fold or expand, so I knew there was enough
more than enough space for the words yet to come.
And within it all that sense of fresh start, making our mark,
and carrying on the intentions of the older man
by threading his life with our life so the story continues
but just moves to a different page or chapter.
All this flooded with brilliant light.
And ripe, so bitterly ripe.

November Fruit

Wild apples warm
in November light. Glowing discs
anoint the tips of branches.
Sunset. Summer set.
As pennies suspended in autumn,
the red-tail caught free-fall.
It's not so much the fracture
as what we do to repair that matters.
First responder: this is your call to beauty.
Copper glows through unplucked fruit.
Winter feed, winter freed
from autumn. I release you.

April, in a Town Full of Fools

The fools were willing to consign
all their parts to the broker.
The broker was fat and well-sated,
the fools empty and hungry.
They traded their parts for bread, a teaspoon of jam,
fresh hay for their beds, schoolbooks for their children.
Not one of the fools ever questioned the contract.
Not one of them challenged the arrangement.
The fools lived out their days diminished, part by part
they were lessened.
In the end the broker moved
to another village, and the town was left full
of thin and wandering fools.

We Are Welcomed Home by the US

in the form of an older cowboy. Hat, boots.
Texas drawl. He's the gateman.
Immigration and Customs.
He directs us to the touch screen
on our left. A few swipes, an iris scan, and we're in.
The US welcomes us home with "Bi-en-veneedos, y'all."
This is the way *we* cross.
It's late and airport quiet.
Customs cowboy asks, "Y'all bring in any fo-ood?"
I shake my head no and we're through.
Saturday night. Check point Houston.

Border Patrol: La doctora sabe

His supervisor called on a Saturday, *el día sagrado*, for working on the Camaro. Engine oil up to his elbows. Scars on the backs of his hands. *La doctora sabe a donde quiere ir, you just have to drive her around.* Something about bones and reunification. Good will and humanitarian cause. *Don't take her too close to the barrels.* She was waiting at the station on Monday. Early, just his luck. *La doctora sabe*, his grandmother said when the baby threw up all night, when his grandfather couldn't stop coughing. A trust he didn't share but never questioned. La doctora worked for hours with barely a break, only a small bottle of water. She spoke of predators and remains, he thought about lunch at the grill. She approached the bones with a whisper. Only a small bottle of water. He didn't mention the names the other guys had for the bodies found by the river. Crushed beer cans, cold coffee, the baby was sick at home. La doctora arrived with a bottle of *remedio* wrapped in a brown paper bag. Bones and reunification. Goodwill and humanitarian cause. Scars on the backs of his hands.

I Am Told They Remained after the War

By then the fig tree was much taller
than Pasquale.

No way back across the ocean
once the fighting began.

Momma was failing,
the garden overrun,

her sisters' complaints
sprouting higher than the tree.

Somehow Pasquale managed
to find a spring brood,

traded eggs for butter, butter for bread.

Poco per volta, *the windows caulked,*
chimney cleaned, new seats for the kitchen chairs.

All those years sailing back and forth across the ocean,
un piede qui e un piede lá,

one foot in the old world, one in the new
and Richetta always on the wrong side.

Like the hen that kept running to the neighbor's yard
pecking the fence,

that relentless desire for change.
One day she ended up in the roaster, ma che.

Richetta knew she would stay,
the figs just coming into season.

The Trees Were Filled with Blossoms but No Bees

it was a season of messengers
—Rachel Blum

It was a season of cracked leather.
The creek ran low. The children were released
from school, the teachers had abandoned their classrooms.

It was a time of unusual migrations.
The mail had stopped, the hospitals considered closing.
It was during this time they met.

They knew it was useless and
that seemed to make it more compelling.

Magnetic, he said.
Electrifying, she.

The earth warmed and the winds
dried out the gardens.
At the beach, sand was disappearing. Waves
crashed over the piers. They walked the narrow
strip of sand, found pieces of boat
motors, splintered oars.

They didn't bother about their stories,
skipped over their *how did you's* and *when did that's*.

Evenings they prepared intricate meals with only a few
ingredients
and marveled at the variations they concocted.

They ate leftovers on the shrinking
beach, carried worn books and read to each other constantly.

Epic stories and how-to manuals,
maybe they would come in handy yet.

On their last day, a lame coyote crossed the road in front of them.
He was considering a new version of supper,
she was thinking, *Maybe we build a boat.*

Mi Estrella, Soñé con tí anoche. Estabas caminando conmigo. Cada rato, tenías que descansar. Poco a poco te retrasabas. Busqué tu mano y solo encontré espinas de cholla. Miré mi mano. Las gotas de sangre se parecían a recién nacidos—sonriéndome y peleándose entre ellos.

NOTES

"Desert Manifest" is inspired by the doctors and many others who assist in the search, retrieval, and identification of human remains found in the Sonoran desert.

"All the Heroes Are Silent" has borrowed lines from Anna Akhmatova and Jessica Dawn Palmer.

"Report from the Undertaker" is a response to the painting by Susan Ferguson titled *Teotihuacan*. Gratitude to Catherine Ferguson for sharing her mother's work.

"Humanitarian Release" is dedicated to Jakelin Caal Maquino, one of the young victims of US immigration and border policy. The italicized lines are borrowed from Ada Limón and translated into Spanish.

"Such Is the Story of Leaving" is dedicated to my husband, Gustavo Seluja.

"Caceroleada" refers to an international tradition of banging household implements, such as wooden spoons and pots, as a form of grassroots protest. This tradition is frequently seen in Latin American countries and was specifically recalled by the author's husband in his country, Uruguay, during the military dictatorship in the 1980s.

"Letter to My Suegra from Artesia, New Mexico" is dedicated to the Seluja family.

"The Function of Walls" has borrowed lines from *Animal Wisdom* by Jessica Dawn Palmer and *Structure and Function in Man* by Jacob Francone Lossow.

"How to Lose One Thousand Four Hundred Seventy-Five Children" relies in part on the 2018 announcement by the Department of Health and Human Services that a significant number of unaccompanied immigrant children had been "lost" to follow-up within the system. This statement was later modified and retracted.

"Unsigned Affidavit" is a response to images of the southern border as seen in the stunning volume *Border Cantos* by Richard Misrach and Guillermo Galindo. The opening line relies on an image described in Valeria Luselli's essay, "Tell Me How It Ends."

"Postmortem Variations" has borrowed lines from *Animal Wisdom* by Jessica Dawn Palmer.

"Consider the Night" is inspired by the quilt titled *Night* by Mary Olivea.

"Lament for Joaquin Macias" references two separate events: the 2017 occurrence of employees of certain Motel 6 hotels, primarily in Arizona and Washington state, illegally forwarding guest lists to ICE for their review, and the earthquake in Mexico City during the same year.

"Cesare's Gift" has lines borrowed from Theodore Roethke.

"To Be Part of Something Complete and Great" is a line borrowed from Willa Cather.

ACKNOWLEDGMENTS

I have so much gratitude for the support that appeared along the road to completing this book, a road that occasionally felt like a superhighway but more often felt like a barely visible animal track scuttling through the trees.

My deepest thanks to the University of New Mexico Press for once again saying yes to my work and believing in the value of getting these poems out into the world. Thanks to Elise McHugh, James Ayers, the entire design and marketing team, and (always) Hilda Raz.

Many of these poems were workshopped in different classes facilitated by Lise Goett, Veronica Golos, Lynn Miller, and Hilda Raz. Thank you.

Thanks to my brother, Tom DiBella, for feedback on the poems, clarifying points of family history, and many long and satisfying discussions on process and art.

Grazie mille a mi paisana and Sicilian translator, Simonetta Rinaldi Trinchieri. So many last minute DMs!

To my trusted circle: Tina Carlson, Catherine Ferguson, Gary Worth Moody, Will Barnes, Stella Reed. I can't imagine this road without you.

To my extended Seluja family for daily showing me the strength and good humor required to keep stepping forward on the path to a new life in a new country.

Gratitude always, always to my ancestors, who kept these family stories alive, especially Serafina Rossi, Edith Rossi Godman, and Irma Rossi DiBella.

To the many, many patients I have cared for over the past forty years, who daily meet the challenge and the struggle of making a new home in a country that sadly says no to them much more often than it says yes.

To the countless individuals and volunteers who work for immigration justice.

Y, a mi amorcito, mi marido Gustavo, who not only assisted with many of the Spanish translations but, more importantly, inspired me to think deeply about a life that spans borders.

CREDITS

The author is deeply grateful to the editors of the following journals in which these poems have appeared, sometimes in slightly different forms:

bosque: "Carciofo" and "In Your Letter You Asked about Ceremony"
Claudius Speaks: "We the Dead"
Cutthroat: "The Trees Were Filled with Blossoms but No Bees"
Duality: "Such Is the story of Leaving," "House Made of Fog and Goodwill," and "We Are Welcomed Home by the US"
The Fourth River: "Freight Train"
Mom Egg Review: "To Be Part of Something Complete and Great"
Naugatuck River Review: "My Grandfather Teaches Me How to Flay the Heart"
New Mexico Poetry Review: "Your Grandmother's Bolognese"
Ovunque Siamo: "On the Day I Order My Ancestry Kit, I Also Order Scopa Cards"
Santa Ana River Review: "Letter to My Suegra from Artesia, New Mexico"
Santa Fe Moment: "The Joy of the Moment Turns Suddenly into a Black Hood with Openings"
Sin Fronteras: "Border Patrol: Por supuesto" and "Mi amorcito"
Taos Journal of International Poetry and Art: "To Be Carried This Way"

"My Grandmother Told the Story This Way" appeared on *The Unruly Muse,* an audio podcast hosted by Lynn C. Miller and John Modaff (Episode 19, "Faith," September 2022, the Creek Studio).
"Monastery in the Desert, Abiquiu, New Mexico" is included in the Santa Fe Telepoem Project.

"November Fruit" is displayed as part of the Taos, New
    Mexico, Poetry in Nature Project at the Helene Wurlitzer
    Foundation.
"Three Studies of an Angel" is part of the Pen Norway Ilhan
    Project.
"Letter to My Suegra from Artesia, New Mexico" is included
    in the anthology *What Saves Us: Poems of Empathy and
    Outrage in the Age of Trump*, edited by Martín Espada
    (Northwestern University Press, 2019).